Tell me, what date was love invented?

Produced by Infinite Imprint, LLC
Edited by Lisa "Zazou" Pierre
Designed by Abraham Auguste
Cover Image by Zeek Mathias

In these pages, you will discover a love that defies physical attributes, a love that binds spirits, and a love that thrives in silent expressions, where our shadows eloquently convey devotions without our consent. It's an organic love that flows unbidden, touching the very core of our souls.

Amidst these verses, you will come to appreciate the significance of loving someone in your silence. It's a love that requires no words, a love that simply exists, nurturing bonds that go beyond what can be articulated. Loving You in My Silence is a testament to the magic of love that exists beyond words, beyond consent, and beyond the surface—a love that whispers in the stillness of your soul and forever leaves its mark on your heart.

LOVING YOU IN MY SILENCE

Table of Contents

I Love You In My Silence	8
Sacred Angel	10
Passage of Time	12
A Muse's Touch	14
Lullaby Kisses	16
Apocalyptic Love	17
Speak Them My Love	18
The Intimacy of My Soul	20
Shadow of Your Smile	22
Language of Musicians	24
I Wonder If He Knows	26
Glass Soul	27
Let Me Ride This Ship	28

Tears of The Raindrops	30
Rose Petals	31
Organic Field	32
When Love Comes	33
Unity	34
Seal Our Faith	35
What Matters Now, Matters in My Dream	36
Confession Of A Lotus Flower	38
Archival Vault of Love	40
Shield Wall	41
11.30.23	42
Seal The Door My Angel	45
The Last Rose Petal	46

Synopsis

This collection of love poems explores the depths of love's profoundness, going beyond surface-level attraction and affection. The collection of poems explores love as a spiritual connection between two souls, transcending physical boundaries. Rather than focusing on romantic cliches, these poems examine the quieter but deeper aspects of love - the implicit understanding between two people, the ability to communicate without words, and the soul bond that exists regardless of circumstance. Love is conveyed not through grand gestures but in subtle looks, gentle touches, and unspoken devotion. The poems highlight love that flows naturally once two hearts are attuned, not forced or performative. Whispered in stillness, this love manifests as a spiritual experience. True love is a reality that doesn't know the boundary of dreams. The poems guide readers to appreciate love's silent reverence, subtle wisdom, and spiritual transcendence. Imagine discovering "A love where our shadows express devotions without our consent because it's organic love."

I Love You In My Silence

I avoid sleep, because sleep disturbs my silence

Saying I love you doesn't bare the weight

Nor is as significant, as my silence

The silence you experience

Is when I am trying to figure out a way to say that I love you,

Without it having neither a beginning nor an end

In my silence, I am constructing and thinking of ways

To when I say that I love you

How to make the rhythm of the sounds of

these words last forever, with no interruptions

The stream lavishes the fragrance of your remarkable beauty

A beauty that reverberates in your silhouette,

that embraces your innocence

A temperament of a lilac flower that flourishes

from a drop of a tear, of a raindrop

Queen like quality

A reflection of divine beauty

I would not ask God for permission

The love within my silence is everlasting,

And only those who belong to the fraternity of immortals,

can understand

I love you, in my silence

When the spirit of love has crumbled to dust and leave my body

Then and only then, will I utter these words

Because then, I know it's the last words that I have whispered

Humbly,

I love you in my silence

Sacred Angel

Sacred Angel of Divinity

Dancing in the shadow of my heart

Humming, hymns of lullaby, to the saints of unity

Let me Be the one that creates the stairs

To the bottom of your heart

To light up the fortune

Within the constellation of your soul

May the inferno, within me

Be sealed with the warmth of your kiss

Let the inquisition of my naked virgin lips

Be free to wonder, where lovers' immortal imaginations

Have yet reached

Libation of mercies, my love

Libation of mercies for my thoughts, my love

For the saints have heard my many prayers at the altar

May the inferno, within me be sealed with the warmth of your kiss

Passage of Time

The passage of time blurs the inner sublimation of Love

So tonight,

I create

Memories of what time has taken from me

The crackling sounds of the candlelight

will cast a shade over the moon

And the hues from the darkness shall prevail

The many layers of the mask will be revealed

And no longer hide what was once considered

a dream Of an organic love

An addiction, not to the nectar

But to the titillation of the honeycomb

where tears of bitter honey, no longer flows

The many vicarious attempts

To feel

To touch

To caress

The emotion collapses at the feet of insanity

For the passage of time is unforgiving

She has no grace

And shows no mercy

Stamped with the curse of unpleasant regrets

The infinite possibilities

The many hours of vows exchanged with solitude

A quest for a soul,

within a lifeless memory of the passage of time

So tonight, I rejoice.

The morning dew, is the residue, of my pain

A Muse's Touch

Felt by the vibration of her sensuality

How far will she let the creativity of my imagination take me?

The path to her divine garden where the

fragrance of the tropics is abundant

The delightful taste of her lips

as she intertwines her hips with my lips

bringing ecstasy to my soul

In an instant, she guides my hand

over the warmth of her body to cuddle my mind

Teaching me the meaning of fate

And how to be obedient to my thoughts of vulnerability

She manifests in my darkest dreams

To align the frequency of our heartbeats

in tune with one infinite motion

The interlocking of unpublished memories

Our emotional language wove in a web of complexity

and the simplicity of a hug

All of my thoughts are embraced

with grace and acceptance

as she bows to my heart's affection

I whisper to her "All I've ever manifested in love,

came in my dreams"

She smiles

The morning dew gently caresses my heart

The sunrise is her cue to depart

I thank her for the mental tuck

as I watch the spirit of the wind carry her away

I open my eyes, thoughts collected,

and bravely grab a pen I ask

Have you ever felt the invisible touch of a muse's vibration?

And, If you have,

Please kneel and help me pray.

Lullaby Kisses

Lullaby kisses, dancing to the silhouette of love

Pecking through the treasures of heaven,

like I only know Oh love, We are lullaby kisses,

dancing to the silhouette of love

Entering the labyrinth of love with no end

Take me, to the chaotic night's journey,

to the witness of the morning dew

Oh love, we are lullaby kisses,

dancing to the silhouette of love

Lead me, where my lips have no compassion

to surrender

Tender mercy, needs no witness

As we explore the beauty of the valley

Oh love we are lullaby kisses,

dancing to the silhouette of love

Tell me, Show me,

Where desires meet dreams

Undress my touches gracefully

Blessed garden, protected by the sweet fragrance of love

Sunrise to sunset, under the curfew of love

Oh Love, we are lullaby kisses,

dancing to the silhouette of love

Apocalyptic Love

Deep within my soul, there's an apocalyptic war raging

The Armageddon of all love

This path filled with emotion, passion,

and fragmented loneliness

Here in my heart, exists a place

where the waves of passion

are hidden in the dungeon of my essence

A life shared by the embrace of our shadows

Manifested with every public encounter

To spare society's discontent inquisitions

Away with the waves of the existence

of my reality–a secret,

That can't be revealed

A complex love hidden within

the labyrinth of our souls

True love is a reality that doesn't know

the boundary of dreams

Awaken!

I realize that I am simply a beneficiary of the vicarious longing of

our shadows' dream

Cry mercy, my love

Cry mercy my divine descent, Cry mercy

Speak Them My Love

Tell me the secrets of your heart

Or have you not the courage

To utter the words

The words that are unifying

Unifying to an inseparable existence

My love, let me speak of this love

This love that is rich with harmony

And Infinite memories, that have yet to come

Guide me with the gleam of your eyes

And your insatiable smile

Come closer

Let me feel thy lips spirited

with umimaginable innocent pleasures

Give me life

Life as it is known to an immortal

I beg of you

To whisper the unspeakable words

That is hidden within the abyss

of your mortal soul

And masqueraded by uncertainty

and echoless emotions

Speak them, my Love

Speak

And I shall be free

The Intimacy of My Soul

The intimacy of my soul

Viewed by the whispers of the hummingbird

Songs of lullaby, for all to hear, for all to see

The intimacy of my soul brings me to life

Then birds of feathers

flocked and scribbled upon darkness

You and I

We and I

And I and us

Why do reasons matter?

When a mass appeals

To an ingratitude of a grateful soul

To pass judgment

Yes, they have visited

The intimacy of my soul

And with each swipe

And with each view

My heart falls into despair

For the intimacy of my soul

Has surrendered

Please click, LIKE!

The intimacy of my soul
brings me to life
Then birds of feathers
flocked and scribbled
upon darkness

Shadow of Your Smile

I want to live in the shadow of your smile

Where angels dance

Where I can feel what you feel

Embrace what you embrace

Endure what you endure

I want to live in the shadow of your smile

So that I could be the one to frown

And endure your pain, so that you may smile

Will you allow me?

Will you let me reside

in the shadow of your smile?

I want to live in the shadow of your smile

Where I feel the silhouette of your embrace

I want to live in the shadow of your smile

To beg for forgiveness

In the shadow of your smile where I know

That love smiles back

I want to live in the shadow of your smile

Where saints lose control

And lose sight of light

Yes, in the shadow of your smile

Where I am at liberty to run free

And I get a chance to be me

Yes, in the shadow of your smile

I want to live

In the shadow of your smile

Language of Musicians

I want to speak the language of musicians

Sacred conversations,

affirmed by nods

Confirmed smile, and intense gaze of acceptance

I want to speak that language

Simple melodies embraced by chords

All, under one sheet

Bless by the sensuality of the presence

Oh God, sweet Jesus

I want to speak the language of musicians

Dance my love

Dance

Close your eyes, and dance

The rhythmic movement of your hips

brings harmony to my soul

Simple minor progressions, yet so dynamic

I want to speak the language of musicians

Slow down the tempo my love

So I can hear the high pitch, the low pitch

All in one score

There is no theory

Just a leap of faith

To this major tune

My love

I want to speak the language of musicians

Will you teach me

I Wonder If He Knows

Papaya, Mango, Pineapple

I wonder if he knows

From a distance, I observe

In the midst of despair

Makes me wonder

If he knows?

Side by side, they sat, bodies lightly brushing

From the corner, I hid in full observation

Reminiscing on the beautifully scented taste

I wonder if he knows?

Condemned to perception, how can it be?

When there's 1 plate and 2 forks

I wonder if he knows?

Glass Soul

Crystal tears dripping from a glass soul

Reflections of the longing for a virtuous, intimacy

I have seen the vanity of the glass slipper

Desperately searching for a soul, a glass soul

Enter fire, a resurrection of life

With every glare of conviction the mirror less, faces ,stares

So the journey continues

In the ban of rays reigns from the sun In search of the road

where the shadow of darkness, turns to light

I have felt the yearning, in my lucid dreams

Then, with my ice hands, your heart is touched

And with the glance, at the sparkle of your eyes

I felt your soul ,your glass soul

Long live the vitality of love

Faith is overdue.

Let Me Ride This Ship

Let me ride this ship,

that is guided by the sentiment of love

Uncertain by the turbulence of emotions

Trying to hold on to the cascade of waves

influenced by the whispers of spirited winds

Can you hear it?

Do you feel it?

Free yourself,

For I am the endless void that will satisfy your thirst

To the passion you so desire

I have no beginning, nor end, but I am the future

To a fruitful love,

if you let yourself, be free

Let me rinse your insatiable yearning

with the sweat that trickles from my heated longing,

Let's ride this ship together that is guided

by the whispering winds

And live a moment that is steered

By the endless sounds, of the stream of the ocean

Pay no attention, to the tears that I shed

They will not waste

Let them unify with the streams of the ocean

So that it prolongs the Love that I have for you

For without you,

I have no strength to steer

Or to live

Tears of The Raindrops

Listen to the tears of the raindrops

It speaks of a language

that only lovers understand

We are refined people

That is what I'm led to believe

But look!

What language do our shadows speak?

With every moment,

they seize the occasion to entertain nature

No facade, No perception, No permission

So, I ask you, madam

What language does your shadow speak?

Rose Petals

I have run out of rose petals

Yet, I'm still searching

I feel the echo of that place

where solitude weeps alone,

And tears turn into a stream of pain

You said you understand me

But don't understand

the importance of me loving you

Not physically, but eternally

For that reason

And that reason alone

I keep the thoughts caged in my mind

There, at last, I know they can be tamed

Organic Field

I want to travel to the organic field

Where virgin thoughts, run free

To the field, where reflections are subdued,

By tears of the morning dew

To the field, where the energetic presence,

Of our love, runs free

I want to travel to the organic field

Where my innocence is forever present

And with a simple touch

With a simple acknowledgment,

I can feel love,

Again

When Love Comes

When love comes

The loss of Virgin breaths are praised

Drunken desires of passion are tamed

The depth of my sorrow masqueraded

And love's demons are rested

Grace and favor, my love

When love comes

My soul rest in peace

Unity

The river flows tonight

For tonight we unite

A unity that suppresses and defies reason

I have been patient

Waiting to be convinced

No offering of yellow roses

But tonight, we unite

The stream of tears is unwarranted

A painful happiness

Our love finally united

Embrace me

Hold my hand

Hold it tighter

Feel the vibration of my heartbeat

It's rhythmic passionate humming,

lowers with every breath

I love you, I love you

I love you

Seal Our Faith

Alas, my love

Inhale and seal our faith

When all the scent of the toxic potion is whispered

away by the fragrance of true love

May the union that symbolizes the passion of tulips

Flourish, within the fields of lilacs

Let's not waste a minute

Let us amend time and set the hourglass

to the hour of love

A lifetime of wishes,

subdued on the moonlight statics

And awaken, by the rays of sunlight,

caressed by the moist morning dew

I alone cannot endure this moment

My love, my heart forever belongs to you

Love over pain

Love over hate

Love over Love

What Matters Now, Matters in My Dream

What matters now

Matters in my dream

A surreal delusion

Living today's dream in yesterday's memory

Not defeated but I will bow

I will beg

I'll kneel before the throne of time

It's almost midnight

Still holding on to a glass slipper made from ice

Slowly melting away all the passion

The lifelong desires

Melting away the senses of emotions

the depth of my love

Is love an illusion?

I dare ask the spirit of Macaria

A fantasy of a beautiful romance

Fighting the thought of time's inequities

The bitterness of time's fairy tales

The absence of time,

when the presence of time,

mattered the most

Any moment now

It's midnight

More tears to fill the ocean

Begging the wings of nostalgic hope to take me away

All that I know, I learned in my dreams

It's 5 a.m.

An invitation stamped with the seal of a lotus flower,

unopened

When all that matters, matters no more

When all that matters, only matters in my dream

Confession Of A Lotus Flower

Arise my love, for you have bloomed

Tears of pearls in this rain of silence

A journey of deep sorrow

Solitude moments filled with emptiness

in the ocean's cloud

Detached by the petals of the red roses

and love realities

Arise love,

for you have endured the brunt of the enferno

You are my strength to the strange feelings manifested

in my dreams,

the more that I accept, the stranger the feelings

In this moment, I feel the thunder of a rage,

I see what others missed,

the mystery of the rose thorns that

surrounded the beauty of the lotus flower,

the diamond hidden within the comfort of a rock in a pond

I have felt the jolt of the lightning , the roar of the thunder,

the mystery of the storm

Yet alone, I love, for heaven is cold

May the demons within me be buried

with the depth of my sorrow

And the mask within reach, I wear alone

Love remains and love will always be.

Archival Vault of Love

Archaic are the thoughts locked in the archival vault

Extreme measures of caution to protect

the tabu of my thoughts

My love, unlock the vault,

guide me with your aura

your sentiments, your sensations

Help me uncover the pleasures of illusion

Take me where the ocean and clouds meet

captivated by the extreme

silence of many moonlit nights

Sunray kisses, radiant touches, extreme grasp

As I simultaneously beg for mercy and forgiveness,

all in the same breath

Unspoken words,

grow and live inside the furnace within me

And in my moment of solitude, I sometimes wonder

Am I the master of this extreme love

or am I simply the subject of this dream?

Shield Wall

Shield wall, my love

Spring is here, and Autumn is to come

A gift of love,

a gift of faith leads to the path,

the path of sanctity

Time, adoration, and destiny entangled

in a wave of devotion

Shield wall my love

and protect me from the sanctity of time

Shield wall my love for the sacrament of love

Shield wall my love,

only after I have entered your heart

Shield wall my love

11.30.23

My shadow dreamt of you last night

And brought the sunlight of the moon

The dimness of the stars

And the purest of archangels

To bear witness

A Sacred Affirmation of Love's dissertation

Tender devotion, Royal affection

And random thoughts of adoration,

A simple consummation of our shadow's union

My shadow dreamt of you last night

Silky curves, Captivating hips

Crafted rosy lips, olive skin, vanilla kisses,

The sweetness of honey

Let me worship you

The vibration of our heartbeats

Its rhythmic hums of passion

Desirable, Delightful

The tenderness of your embrace

Let me worship you

My shadow dreamt of you last night

And in my dream,

Water, wind, air, and fire surrendered to time

As if space didn't exist

When the sunlight of the moon

The dimness of the stars

The purest of archangels

And the Gods of all Gods asked me,

"Are you in love?"

I simply answered,

Look at the tears of our shadows

Even shadows have dreams

*Love's wraith contained in the
fortress of hope
Yet my soul remains pure*

Seal The Door My Angel

Seal the door my angel with the lantern of faith

For heaven's gate has the residues of divine ashes

Love's wraith contained in the fortress of hope

Yet my soul remains pure

Barefoot imprints of heartbeats

remind me that love's curfew is invisible to time

An internal duel waxed with dimmed soot

Be merciful my angel,

Be merciful and seal my faith

The Last Rose Petal

Aisles of ivory white orchids

Disguised in a scented bouquet of dreams

An imaginary fragrant of colorful kisses

A tribute to the last rose petal

A declaration of a union not yet perfected

The intertwined vines above the surface

have not quite bloomed

Yet the roots below exchanged vows

with solitude many moons ago

A cosmic connection, as witnessed by the lotus flower

The Exotic thoughts that seeped from a hug

Thought of, as the end of submerged thoughts

When the thoughts were truly

the genesis of the manifestation of true love

Begging to be rescued

Grant mercy, my love

I could have watered you more

With grace and gratitude

We shall cross paths again

As our journey on love's timeline has yet to bloom